TESTIFY

TESTIFY

SIMONE JOHN

OCTOPUS BOOKS

PORTLAND, SEATTLE, DENVER

FOR
GARY JOHN, JR.
AND EDWARD SWAIN

FOR
THE FAMILIES OF THOSE NAMED
IN THIS COLLECTION: MAY YOUR
LOVED ONES REST IN POWER

NOTES

ACKNOWLEDGMENTS

FOR THE RECORD, I RECOGNIZE I AM EASILY PREY.

KENDRICK "K. DOT" LAMAR

ORDER OF EVENTS

We started talking about the All-Star Game,
him tellin me to go check for him if it's on.
It wasn't. The game started at 7:30PM.
In perfect pitch Mary J. Blige asked,
Does that star spangled banner yet wave?
The crowd clapped in response.
Ne-Yo closed the half-time show:
For all we know, we might not get tomorrow
Let's do it tonight

But the call dropped at 7:16. Then: sirens.
Windows washed in red light. Occupants
peering through parted curtains, watching
EMTs lift the limp wrist of a stranger
in the street. Elsewhere, brown boys
sat around the screen, waiting
for the game to begin.

HE SAID

What did you and Mr. Martin talk about?

The All-Star Game.

The All-Star Game meaning what, the basketball game?

The All-Star basketball game, it was happening that day.

Then what happened?

And then he said, "Nigga is still following me now."

    I can't hear you.

"That— nigga— is — still — following — me — now."

HOW THE MAN LOOK LIKE

—*He—Mr. Martin—complained? What was he complaining about?*

—That a man kept watching him.

—*After he said that, did you say anything back to him, or did he say anything back to you?*

—Yes, I had asked him how the man look like. And he just told me the man looked creepy—

—*You said the man looked creepy?*

—Creepy, white, s'cuse my language, cracker.

—*They're having trouble hearing you, so take your time—*

—I had asked him how the man look like. He said, "He look like a creepy ass cracker."

—*Okay. Lemme make sure we got that: creepy ass cracker. Is that what you recall him say—*

—Yes.

—*And by that, you mean, a white individual?*

EASY STREET REALTY HAIBUN

The Retreat at Twin Lakes islovely place to call home. Gorgeous town home in gated complex with resort-style pool and clubhouse, ponds, great community amenities. Covered back porch to quiet yard with no facing neighbors, ready for a barbeque. Convenient to major commutes and employers. Near Town Center Mall, great restaurants and shopping. Take in the clubs, entertainment and music at Historic Sanford's new waterfront area and marina. Like the water? Enjoy boating and world-class fishing on nearby Lake Monroe and the St Johns River. Lovely home in a convenient location, waiting for you to make it yours.

THE PICTURES: COLOR

SATURATED. PHOTOSHOPPED

FUTURE. QUIET STREET.

IT MIGHTA BEEN A RAPIST

What did you say to him? Or what did he say to you after that?

Well, he told me the man was lookin at him, so I had to think, it mighta been a rapist.

I'm sorry. I didn't hear the answer.

—Okay, she's going to repeat it. Can you please repeat your answer?

Go ahead. I'm sorry, Madame Court Reporter, please tell me when you're ready.

I'm ready.

Go ahead then, repeat your answer. What else did you say to him and what did he say to you?

"Nahhh, stop playin around wit me like dat."

"Stop playing around with him like that?"

Yeah.

He, Mr. Trayvon Martin, told you to stop playing around with him like that,
as in stop joking with him like that?

Yeah.

And then what happened next?

I told him, "Okay, then why he keep lookin at you?"

CODA

To be a person in a woman's body:
lurking strangers always hold
the possibility of rape.

THEN WHAT HAPPENED

—And then I said, 'Trayvon' and I heard him say 'Why are you following
   me for?' And I heard a hard-breathing man say, 'Whatchu doin
   round here?'

—*Then what happened?*

—I was callin, 'Trayvon, Trayvon, what's goin on?' And I started hearin him
   say, 'Get off, get off.'

—*Then what did you hear?*

—Suddenly the phone hung up. The phone shut off.

BACK SEATS

We know we age in dog years. Seen friends'
lives bookended by brackets before turning 21.

We wonder out loud about lives we'll lead *if*
we grow up, not when we grow up.

We wear the faces of the fallen on our t-shirts
leave favorite fitted caps in their caskets.

We savor our youth knowing
midlife ended in middle school

That the sum of our life might
be summer nights in a back seat.

THE WAKE, THE FUNERAL

—*Why didn't you go to the wake and to the funeral?*

—I didn't wanna see the body.

—*You spoke to his parents, his mother and father?*

—Yes.

—*Did you end up lying about why you didn't go to the wake, the funeral?*

—Yes.

—*Why did you lie about why you didn't go to the wake, the funeral?*

—I felt guilty.

—*Guilty about what?*

—That I was the last person that talked to they son. And I didn't go to the wake, didn't show no respect.

MISSED CALLS

—*When the phone shut off, what happened then?*

—I called him back.

—*So you called Trayvon Martin back—were you able to talk to him again?*

—No.

—*Did he, Trayvon Martin, ever call you back?*

—No...

—*Did you ever talk to Trayvon Martin again?*

—No.

TRAYVON

I've written around
him, poem pieces scaffold-
ing an unnamed loss.

This is the first, last,
only time I'll address this
specter by his names.

First: peer. Aged too close
for comfort. Weekends spent watch
-ing the same cartoons

from different couches.
Both someone's younger sibling.
Someone's youngest child.

Next: brother. See, I've
got one of those too. I've watched
him stumble around

setbacks strewn in front
of him. Navigate a path
littered with landmines.

Fall prey to baited
traps. Some boys can overcome,
but that requires

the luxury of
time. Here there's brevity in
each stanza—always

three lines, and always
of seventeen syllables.
That number now holds

new meaning, suggests
abbreviation— a life
severed at the quick.

MISSED BEATS:
GOOD KID, M.A.A.D CITY

When K. Dot dropped *Good Kid, M.A.A.D City*
it debuted at number two. Most of us
had been stealing the album piecemeal
downloading leaked singles
hungry for the whole thing.

When K. Dot dropped Good Kid, M.A.A.D City
your body had been cold for six months.
Each time I hear him say, *It's deep rooted*
the music of being young and dumb
Each time I rap Backstreet Freestyle
in the mirror before going out, I think
about how you should be somewhere
doing this, too.

FROM

from (frəm) *prep.*

BENJAMIN CRUMP
RACHEL JEANTEL

1.) Indicating the point in space at which a journey, motion, or action starts :
You can't compartmentalize injustice. The only way to understand it is to
trace its gnarled roots from the beginning. 2.) Indicating the point in time
at which a particular process, event, or activity starts: *Q :* Is your family
from where? *A :* Haiti and Dominican; Her reply: a country and an ethnicity.
Questions asked backwards, answered sideways. If it were up to her, K.
Dot would cross-examine the examiner: *"Man down—where you from,
nigga? Fuck who you know, where you from my nigga?"* 2a.) Indicating
the distance between a particular place and another place used as a point
of reference : The land her family hails from is steeped in resistance—but
it couldn't be further from here. 3.) Indicating one extreme in a range of
conceptual variations : People of color are over persecuted on crimes from
routine traffic stops to murder. The number of New York black boys stopped
and frisked exceeds the number of black boys in the city. 4.) Indicating a
distinction : She sat stonefaced and nineteen, trying on adulthood against her
will. Yet the court viewed her as different from her peers. Black children age
in dog years.

SMALL TALK

I.

Well, since they are both sub human
and they didnt have language skills
until the arabs gave them a language;
I would say the feral groids are
reverting back to their natural state
of incomprehensibility.

II.

Good grief, how did Trayvon
even have a conversation
with this girl? She has trouble
stringing more than a few words
into a sentence.

III.

I couldn't get past those huge earrings.

RACHEL'S EARRINGS

I brush her cheek as she shakes her head:
No, he never called back. A gesture of comfort

like seeing a sign written in your mother tongue
while traveling in a foreign land. I hang

at shoulder height, dangling from an ear titled
toward a question doubling back on itself:

Are you saying that you rushed through it
and you didn't think about it carefully

enough to be sure that you told it accurately?
I watched from the dresser this morning

as she held her own gaze in the mirror
hands skimming the jewelry box

seeking armor, seeking anything
to make her brave.

TALLY OF INTERRUPTIONS

In the first fifteen minutes
Rachel is stopped mid
sentence sixteen times.
I'm frustrated with the pauses
requests for repetition.
The typists' audible huff
takes the place of punctuation:
I didn't hear the answer.
Can you repeat that?
I can't hear you.
Mild comments delivered
with a chiding tone.
The disembodied voice
of a woman off camera
unable to conceal her irritation
as a girl recounts the sounds
of her friend's death.
Her voice muffled like
his last breath.

RACHEL JEANTEL

ANY DAY OF THE WEEK

Friday feels like it left
a month ago, though
the way they all go on about
what they did, and who with,

you'd think it just happened.
I would trade Tuesday
for Thursday in a heartbeat
but no one's offering. Shit

I'd even take a Sunday—that
halfhearted weekender—over
today. On Monday mornings
lips work overtime

to keep the rumor mill in motion.
If someone gave me a ticket
outta here, I'd take it
any day of the week.

ON WATCHING RACHEL

White folks only appreciate AAVE
if it's autotuned to a diluted
MetroBoomin beat, with a catch phrase
they can repeat out of context.
Awkwardly inserting *Ain't nobody
got time for that* into casual conversation.

Unconcerned with the fire Sweet Brown
fled, or the abductor dwelling next to
Charles Ramsey, or the teen girl
on the witness stand recounting
her friend's final words. Like black
pain is a joke and the audience
is waiting for the punchline.

NO FURTHER QUESTIONS

—*Ms. Jeantel since that time, have you heard the telephone recording where there's cries for help and then a shot? Have you heard that on TV and stuff?*

—Yes.

—*Okay. The cries for help—are you able to say whose voice that is?*

—Trayvon. It sound like Trayvon's.

—*I don't have any further questions, thank you.*

MOURNING RITES
(OR: HOW WE BURY YOUR SON)

Gather his sneakers from each corner of the house.
Bury them at the basketball court. Cut the net
from the rim and place it in your purse.
When the sound of Jays on concrete
makes a sob crawl up your throat, finger

the nylon like prayer beads. Recite his middle name
until it sounds like a chant. When his favorite cereal
goes on sale, buy a box for every song
you'll never dance to at his wedding.
On Sundays, listen to voicemails he left you

like hymnals. Fold his unfinished homework
into a paper plane. Carry it in your wallet
until receipts rub math problems to dust.
Start collecting souvenir bibs for children
who will never call you grandma.

Did you expect them to understand
what it means to be a one-woman jazz funeral
to sway to a brass band no one else can hear?
They have never known what to make of your mourning.

446

Ranch-style, raised like every other house on the block;
Pine-Sol on Saturday mornings; Psalms on Sundays;
"Don't make me come down there" bumping against bared
teeth; seasonal decorations; black santas and snowfall;
abandoned fort in the woods; *"You need to learn how to
fight—hold your fists like this—no, this—don't tell mom I
told you;"* bunk beds offering the illusion of space; shared
room; shared womb; names written on the wall (in pencil,
erasable to ward off whoopins); 'God books' stacked on
the coffee table, bible on the bottom, devotional on top;
prayers said in hushed tones, for reasons I was too young to
understand; *God grant me the serenity to accept the things I
cannot change* chanted into the cordless kitchen phone.

TWENTY-FIVE PERCENT

A story as old as plantation platitudes:
Married white man sleeps
with teenage black girl
But this was no slave time statistic.

For starters, the scene was set
in New York in the fifties; the teen
my grandmother.
Decades later this infidelity

became classroom currency:
I'm Italian you know
twenty-five percent—
angling for legitimacy.

The beads on my braids clanked
as I nodded for emphasis.
I spent the rest of recess
invoking a stranger

whose name I did not know
whose face my father would never see.

RED LINE

The Red Line pulses through my origin story
like lifeblood. Ashmont to Alewife.
My father ironing his uniform in silence
before driving to the train yard at dusk.
I come from blue collars and barbecues.
Mattapan High Speed Trolley rattling
behind my grandma's backyard

where I got my cheeks pinched
by neighbors who knew not to miss
Katie's fish fry up on Cummins.
If you're passing by on the second Saturday
in June and you hear Marvin Gaye singing
from the sidewalk, come make yourself a plate.
The gate is never locked.

THAT ASS

Black leggings cling to the curves of that ass;
Work out every day just to firm up that ass.

She quickens her pace, counts sidewalk cracks
Hums to muffle *Ma, lemme get at that ass.*

Men's hoodies are the perfect size for hustling
through school hallways, tryna cover that ass.

Just then the DJ drops the bass, them girls
can't keep up with the pace of that ass.

Her palm met his cheek when his hand
landed, uninvited, on the arch of that ass.

Hips pinched while Nana sucks her teeth,
You sho yo momma's daughter, just look at that ass.

NEVER FORGET

Never forget the
lives lost in Pearl Harbor, or
the innocents slain

in concentration
camps, or the people warring
abroad for freedom.

Forget the lashes
lacerating black flesh, the
gashes deep enough

to cradle a grown
man's hands — separate inlets
for every finger.

Forget the boys your
brother's age, affixed to tree
limbs like pendulums

marking passing time.
Forget forefathers tortured
for sport. Forget fore

mothers fearing foot
steps after nightfall, a belt
unbuckled and re

buckled in the dark.
A woman left unzipped. While
you're at it, forget

legacies of black
families fractured for profit.
Forget black bodies

bearing dollar signs.
Forget that those bodies still
mean dollar signs. Whole

industries built to
sell black cool in a country
founded on black backs.

LETTER TO WHITE PEOPLE

I'm not saying you led a lynch mob in a past life.
I'm not disputing the existence of your black best friend,
discounting your grade school MLK report,
or accusing you of siding with the Confederacy.

I'm saying that there's a time and a place
for everything. A conversation about slavery
isn't the best moment to discuss your family's
post-Ellis Island hardships.

I'm saying that you are not entitled
to information about every person
of color who crosses your path.
Including (but not limited to):

Where they're *really* from,
how they get their hair to *do that*,
or their parent's ethnic origins.

I'm saying that boy in school,
the one they called Black Mike?
He grew up to be an adult.

He remembered that class
long after you forgot.

NIGGA DU JOUR

Everyone wants to be the nigga du jour
For the price of a hoodie, a bandana, a chain
You too can have a slice of the black experience
Co-opt the Harlem Shake; leave Stop and Frisk for the rest of us

For the price of a hoodie, a bandana, a chain
Black men get pulled over on side streets
You co-opt twerking; leave tenements for the rest of us
Do you know what it feels like to be hunted?

Black men get gunned down on side streets
By those that serve and protect
Do you know what it feels like to be hunted?
Pursued as pastime

By those that serve and protect?
We've spent centuries
Pursued as pastime
But by all means, buy your "ghetto" Halloween costume

We've spent centuries
Stalked by stereotypes
By all means, buy your "ghetto" Halloween costume
Wooly wigs, smeared red lips, burnt cork for black skin

I am still stalked by stereotypes
But you too can have a slice of the black experience
Wooly wigs, smeared red lips, burnt cork for black skin
See? Everyone wants to be the nigga du jour.

ERASURE

Detox until every ounce of black
is purged from the system.
Start with the nose, unmistakable
even in profile, pronounced bulb
on the tip presiding over the face.

Move to the lips: pantone pink
concealing teeth   pure white or
adorned with gold caps. Elsewhere
ashy skin becomes further evidence
of erasure. A being reduced to dust
the residue that remains after burning.

Purge history of inconvenient achievements.
Draw Malcolm as a terrorist. Dress Martin as a saint.
Disregard the part where he said that *a riot
is the language of the unheard*.
Preach peace at the exclusion of anger.

Populate your media with white people.
Siphon black humanity through exclusion.
Make a movie set in a New York City
that is inexplicably void of black people.

No black patrons in the grocery store,
no black pedestrians on the sidewalk.
If you must include one, justify their presence
with a sassy catch phrase, a murderous agenda.
Edit the scene until the black
at the edges vanishes from view.

RORSCHACH TEST

ON JUNE 14, 2014, JASON HARRISON, A MENTALLY ILL BLACK MAN WAS SHOT TO
DEATH BY POLICE AFTER HIS MOTHER CALLED 9-1-1 FOR ASSISTANCE IN
BRINGING HIM TO THE HOSPITAL.

After the fifth shot was fired
After his body slumped in the doorway
After his mother screamed, *They killed my child*
for the second time. After blood bloomed

Rorschach blots on his white tee, an officer
asks, *He's still alive — should we cuff him?*
The video lingers on a near-lifeless man
mouth moving like a trout on land.

I wonder what the cops see
when they look at him. How is it possible
to watch a man die in his own driveway
and still perceive a threat?

Beyond the frame, there is a mother
who looks at this man and sees birthday
parties. Christmas mornings. A boy
born imbalanced. How quickly the fear

that made her call the police
grew to a fear for her son's life.
Four decades of motherhood
reduced to writhing on concrete.

A cop calls for back up.
He was coming at us, he says
aware of the camera on his uniform.
We had to shoot.

WIDOWS

Prisons widow our women like the grim reaper.
Grandma with no sons to speak of waiting
at the window for the ride to arrive. Carry her
to South Bay Correctional to visit her grandson's ghost.

Her block is occupied by armed forces.
Her address book filled with phone numbers
for other widows. Their husbands all decades dead,
Sending meager checks from beyond the grave.
Each widow raising someone else's child,

Each child orphaned by similar circumstance.
If I called her something other than nana
called her soldier's wife, army mom
said her sons were stolen by war
would her grief matter to you?

When combat wipes out generations of men,
what is left of the women who outlive them?
When husbands and sons and grandsons are gone
who comes back to pull their mothers from the rubble?

THE RULES

When you are born, I will be faced with a choice:
raise a fearless boy to be buried young
or raise a man constantly reminded
of his place. I will tread this tightrope,

teach you the rules. There are things
you cannot do. You cannot
be reckless like your paler peers.
Do not run in public.

Passersby feel prompted to wonder
who you're running from or
where you're running to. Keep nothing
in your hands.

Your hands are the stuff of magic
tricks. What was bought appears
stolen. A snack shapeshifts
into a weapon.

One day you will ask where we came from.
I will pull out a map of Boston, point
at neighborhoods still scarred from forced
busing. Trace my finger along avenues

that serve as mini Mason Dixon lines.
I will pass over the park where my father stood
a year older than you, wiping
another boy's spit from his cheek.

Nigger still ringing in his ears.
And before that you'll ask. I will fumble
for an appropriate response, summon
an image of the sharecropping South

My grandmother with a suitcase on her lap
looking for the last time at a body
lynched limp on sturdy branch.
We'll take turns laughing at Nana's funny phrases:

Lawd amercy, it must not be but fo' degrees outside
I'll explain how her accent followed her from the South.
You'll ask if we can go down there someday
Someday I'll say. Someone should know

where you are at all times. I'm not naïve
enough to think it will be me.
But this rule provides the alibi
you never thought you'd need.

Eventually you'll develop
an inner compass to navigate
this path. I am laying the path
to keep you alive long enough to get there.

CALLS HOME

There are things you don't discuss
on the phone. My father's words
come through the receiver
in a coded tongue; I respond in kind.
I say I just spoke to my brother.
We trade slivers of the story
court dates and contraband,
search warrants police neglected
to furnish. My father elliptically explains
the parallels between them.
How he, at twenty-seven, was snared
in the same wrong things
for the same wrong reasons.
How he, in his twenty-seventh December,
found himself in the same situation.
We loosen our language, exchange
dismayed headshakes in silence
until domesticity calls him to the task
I interrupted. I wonder if,
thirty years from now, my brother
will end a call with his daughter
fetch the mower from the shed
and cut the grass around his home.

TWIN BEDS

For years we slept in bunk beds
first stacked in the corner, then split

and set on opposite sides
of a single wall. Then separated

by a staircase, a hallway, later
replaced by streets, time zones.

My father says he still recalls
putting us to sleep in separate cribs

only to wake and find one empty
the other doubly occupied.

THE CURRENCY OF CHILDHOOD

Nights near forgotten, Nana's living room
with a gang of cousins betting quarters
on their twin of choice, crowding
us like men around pit bulls.

Where the coffee table should have been, we stood
swinging weak fists at one another, knowing
we were a two-girl tribe on the outskirts
of this band of boys.

The group dissolved when crying
started or keys were heard in the door.
The currency of childhood exchanged
between the first people you learned to love.

UNCLE EDDIE

FOR EDWARD SWAIN

Nana's house is a museum of family photos:
snapshots of cousins suspended in time
crooked teeth smiles and corduroy.
Forever five years old, despite pictures
of their own children on the opposite wall.
Grade school photos spanning sixty years
of siblings and kids, and kid's kids.

A house with this much history needs
a steward. Someone solid to anchor the family
when the patriarch passed too soon. A mild
mannered man to steady the ship
against the tumult of life's storms.

In his room, he kept his own photo collection.
Cherry-picked favorites from among
the images wallpapering the living room.
Each sibling, each niece, each nephew
represented in the curated showcase
behind closed doors.

Who knew there was wall for all of us
in his small room, that he held us all so close
without our knowing? Who knew one man
could have a heart big enough to house so many?

SWINGING

Our father outgrew his rage
by the time we were ten.
Before that we thought
it was a game. Pieces
of phones hurled from the porch
were gathered and brought
to the wooded clubhouse.
We'd sit on fallen logs
one hand on an imagined
steering wheel, the other
cradling a faux car phone.

Sometimes we sat on the swing set
he built and practiced cursing.
Shit! Motherfucker! Goddamnit!
Son of a bitch! Fuck! We tried
to feign anger but each word
was punctuated with laughter.
Our legs pumped, voices raised
the higher we went. Too consumed
with our play to notice the screen door
swinging by its hinge.

STREETLIGHT SUTRA

I walked toward
the train, body wrapped
in red wine warmth.
He headed towards me
with a swagger all his own
courtesy of some substance.

Our paths cross under a spill
of lamplight. We each maintain
sloppy gaits without pause.
His voice splits the silence
Stay black and stay blessed
Words crackle like they crossed
radio waves to reach me.

The Oakland air swept away
the slurs of his s's. I heard
wisdom underneath. Nodded
and kept nodding after
he passed. Rolled the phrase
across my tongue. *Stay black
and stay blessed*. Hummed it
into a hymn.

UNBECOMING LANGUAGE

I grew up nursed on curse words.
All the soap in the world couldn't wash
Mattapan out of my daddy's mouth.
Corner boy slang steeped at sea
on a Navy stint to set him straight.

My DNA is explicit. Coded in ampersands
and asterisks. Semi-colons and dollar signs.
An origin story with missing pieces
blurry if you look too close.

My mother tongue is spoken between
gritted teeth full of phrases like:
This motherfucker right here!
Ain't that about a bitch! And sometimes
my poems need to say some shit.

I cannot not say nigga. All my words have edges
and I am built of too many sharp corners.
I am undeterred by your wincing. Unwilling
to change my tone. Always muttering
these motherfuckers under my breath.

COLLATERAL

ARS POETICA

Sandra's words live here without
the cushion of quotation marks.
No asterisks. No caveats. No need.
Black rage cannot be reworded.

A poem cannot be paraphrased.
The meaning has been distilled until
only the right words remain. Until
there is no room for ambiguity.
If attention is a form of prayer

these poems are psalms
for slaughtered women.
Stanzas built of names
excavated from footnotes,
from collateral collected
carefully for preservation.

The poem asks you to slow down.
Pay attention for a few lines.
You look for an excuse to stop,
do anything else, but find nothing.
Now it is too late. Now you
are burdened with knowing.

ELEGY FOR DEAD BLACK WOMEN #1

The first death comes by
bullet. The second, when they've
forgotten your name.

CIGARETTE

—OFFICER ENCINIA
—SANDRA BLAND

—You mind putting out your cigarette, please? If you don't mind?

—*I'm in my car, why do I have to put out my cigarette?*

—Well you can step on out now.

—*I don't have to step out of my car.*

—Step out of the car.

—*No, you don't have the right.*

—Step out of the car.

—*You do not have the right to do this.*

—I do have the right, now step out or I will remove you.

—I refuse to talk to you other than to identify myself. I am getting removed
for a failure to signal?

—Step out or I will remove you. I'm giving you a lawful order. Get out of
the car now or I'm going to remove you.

ON [NOT] WATCHING THE VIDEO

I have seen it posted and re
posted. Always the same still:
officer leaning with his hands
against the roof of her car, legs
spread, head tilted to unleash
his ire into her cracked window.
I too have been bitten by the bark
of a white man's voice. I've dared

someone to touch me, sworn on my life.
Felt the phrase "don't make me" hanging
over me like a punch about to land.
I cannot press play without seeing
my reflection in her rearview mirror.
Without feeling my thighs sticking
to her seat with sweat. My chest braced
by the seat belt. Hand reaching for phantom
cigarettes. Mouth parched with waiting.

A BRIEF HISTORY OF MURDER

The last black girl they killed wore beads in her hair
on picture day. Her name is swallowed instead of spoken.
Her hash tag—trending until they kill the next black boy.

The next black girl they'll kill is writing this poem.

The first black boy they killed was neither black nor boy.
Seen as some rare breed of African wildlife
to be captured. To be carried across the Atlantic.
To be sacrificed to the sea when his body broke
in the belly of the ship. The first black boy
they killed had a mother.

The last black boy they killed had a mother, too. She is
crying into the camera. Sitting on stage with a sorority
of sonless women. They welcome her to the club she didn't
ask to join. Daily, my mother prays not to join. I don't
believe in her god but my poems pray too, in the way poems do.

The next black boy they'll kill is sitting in my classroom
passing notes to the pretty girl who always does her work.

The next black boy they'll kill is my older or younger brother, my cousin.

The next black girl they'll kill is driving with the windows down.

Obeying traffic laws. Listening to a man on the radio talk
about the last black boy. Trying to get home while she
is still whole. Trying not to flinch at the sound of sirens.

INCITING INCIDENT: WHAT'S WRONG

—*Do you have a driver's license? Okay, where you headed to now? Okay, ma'am. You okay?*

—I'm waiting on you. This is your job. I'm waiting on you. When're you going to let me go?

—*I don't know, you seem very irritated.*

—I am. I really am. I feel like it's crap what I'm getting a ticket for. I was getting out of your way. You were speeding up, tailing me, so I move over and you stop me. So yeah, I am a little irritated, but that doesn't stop you from giving me a ticket.

—*Are you done?*

—You asked me what was wrong, now I told you.

FOR COLORED GIRLS WHO HAVE BEEN ASKED "WHAT'S WRONG"

FOR ALISHA DANIELS FROM MISFITS

As if being born a woman
wasn't difficult enough.
As if men need another excuse
to feel entitled to my body.
My body was contested territory
long before that strange storm
turned my skin into
another word for desire.
By 9th grade boys thought
their hands belonged on my hips.
Mike Marrow. Prom date turned sour.
Man-boy with something to prove
behind the gym at school.
Testosterone curdling his blood
while he tells me he *Can't help himself,*
especially in a dress like that. Hair pulled
back in an intricate up-do. My looks
have always been my undoing.
This is why I am sharp wit

with forked tongue.
This is why I am pretty face
pinched into mean mug.
Defense mechanisms
sharpened to protect
a power I never asked for.

LAWFUL ORDERS:
AN ABBREVIATED LIST

OFFICER ENCINIA

Get out of the car now

or I'm going to remove you.

I'm going to yank you out of here.

You are under arrest.

I said get out of the car.

I'm giving you a lawful order.

I'm going to drag you out of here.

I will light you up!

Get

out

now.

ELEGY FOR DEAD BLACK WOMEN #2

Miriam Carey.
Shelley Frey. Aiyana Jones.
Rekia Boyd. Pick

a name you didn't
know. Carry it with you. Bear
the weight of her loss.

A MUCH MORE COMMON TERM

White people use nigga as shorthand
for *I'm still mad I can't own you.*
The word they reach for
when the fear flickering
in their mouths has been kindled
to a flame big enough to swallow Baltimore.

White people use nigga as a proxy
for the word worthless
like a black body is a crash
test dummy, humanlike but hollow.

In their quest for efficiency
white people have boiled hate
into these five letters. Why waste words
when you only need one?

White people use nigga like a nickname
for Freddie Gray and Mike Brown
Aura Rosser and Natasha McKenna
MLK and Obama
Jordan Davis and Emmett Till
Usaamah Rahim and Terrence Coleman
Joyce Quaweay and Korryn Gaines

and

and

and

UNANSWERED QUESTIONS

SANDRA BLAND

When're you going to let me go?
I'm in my car, why do I have to put out my cigarette?
Why am I—
Am I getting removed for a failure to signal?
Ok, so you're going to yank me out of my car?
I'm under arrest—for what?
Why am I being apprehended?
So you're threatening to drag me out of my own car?
You're doing all this for a failure to signal?
You feelin good about yourself?
You feel real good about yourself, don't you?

Why am I being arrested?
Why can't you—
Why am I being arrested?
Why can't you tell me that part?
Why won't you not tell me what's going on?
Are you fucking kidding me?
Are you fucking serious?
You want me to sit down now?

Or are you going to throw me on the floor?
Would that make you feel better about yourself?
I'm getting a warning? For what? For what?!
Do I feel like I have anything on me that's illegal?
You're about to break my wrist—can you stop?

Don't it make you feel good, Officer Encinia?
Don't it make you feel real good?

LAWFUL ORDERS: AFTERMATH

OFFICER ENCINIA

You started creating problems.
Come over here. Stop now!
If you would stop resisting.
Get on the ground.
You are yanking around.
When you pull away from me,
you're resisting arrest.
Good. Good.
I want you to wait right here.
For a warning, you're going to jail.

A WOMAN'S PERSPECTIVE

UNIDENTIFIED FEMALE OFFICER

Stop resisting ma'am.
You should not be fighting.
You should have thought about it
before you started resisting.
Listen to how he is telling you
to get up. Yes you can.
I saw everything.

ELEGY FOR DEAD
BLACK WOMEN #3

FOR THE EMANUEL AFRICAN METHODIST EPISCOPAL
CHURCH IN CHARLESTON, SOUTH CAROLINA

Susie Jackson and
Cynthia Marie Graham Hurd
and Ethel Lee Lance.

Names that sound like my
nana's friends. I can hear them
whisper *Hush, chile. Hush.*

THINGS I DON'T SAY TO THE WHITE AUDIENCE AT THE POETRY READING

I am not your wet nurse, your mammy
your nanny. I am not here to sing
you to sleep. You want a poem
that saunters toward you like your
childhood dog. Places its head
in your lap, waiting to be pet.

I never had a dog. And if I did
my poems would still bloat
with black girl grief
still read like an index of sorrow
still bathe you in the shadow
of a nightmare you never knew to fear.

There is no redeeming nature metaphor here.
No plot twist to leave you feeling lighter.

Just more names
you have already forgotten.
Just more bodies.

ONLY EVERYTHING I OWN

This body is everything I own.
Built like my mother's before it.
Nana's nose. Italian heritage
muted in my making speaks in whispers
in wisps of too-straight hair on my neck.

This body is a compressed continent.
It will never be taller than 5'2
never take up more space than this.
What do you see in me that you wish
to suffocate?
What about this figure says threat?
What about my being unsettles you?

You settled here, uninvited. Black women
brought here for our hardiness
for our ability to carry black babies —
our wombs, the factories that kept fields
full of black men.

Black women are collateral damage.
The body between the bullet
and the person of interest.

Former girlfriend. Unnamed victim.
Mother of a child, now motherless.

This body is only everything I own.
An island you keep trying to conquer.

ELEGY FOR DEAD BLACK WOMEN #4

AN INVOCATION FOR BLACK TRANSWOMEN MURDERED IN THE UNITED STATES

When they hunt you with
abandon and misname you
while mourning, my own

fragile freedom is
hollowed. Wilted. Now, I will
call you queen, call you

cousin, homegirl or
sister-friend. I will conjure
your grace in poems.

I will weave your names
into prayer: Elisha
Walker, Shade Schuler

Keyonna Blakeney
Veronica Banks Cano
Kendarie Johnson

India Monroe
Jazz Alford, Goddess Diamond
and Rae'Lynn Thomas

Ashton O'Hara
Dee Whigham, Deeniquia Dodds
and Papi Edwards

Brandi Bledsoe, Bri
Golec, Kristina Gomez-
Reinwald, Maya Young

London Chanel, Skye
Mackabee, Keisha Blidge
and Jasmine Collins

I TRIED

OFFICER ENCINIA, ON THE PHONE
WITH HIS SUPERIOR

This is a traffic stop, had a little bit of an incident.
I tried to de-escalate her. It wasn't getting anywhere, at all.
I mean I tried to put the Taser away. I tried talking to her
calming her down, and that was not working. I tried to get her
detained and get her to just calm down. Stop throwing her arms.
You know what? She never swung at me, just flailing

and stomping around. I said alright that's enough
and that's when I detained her. I was just trying
to get her out, over to the side and just explain
what was going on because I couldn't even get her
to do what I was telling her.

Like I said, with something like this, I just call you immediately
after I get to a safe stopping point. No weapons, she's in handcuffs.
You know, I only took enough force as seemed necessary. I de-escalated
once we were on the pavement, you know on the sidewalk.
So I allowed time. I'm not saying I just threw her to the ground.
I allowed time to de-escalate and so forth. It just kept getting—

Right, I'm just making that clear. I got some cuts on my hand
I guess that's an injury, but I don't need medical attention.
I got three little circles from the handcuffs
when she was twisting away from me.
Over a simple traffic stop. I don't get it. Really, I don't.
Why they act like that, I don't know.

DANEZ SMITH

BURNING

Cataloguing these killings
turned me into something

not-human. Part poem.
Part funeral pyre.

And who wants to talk to the girl
who only speaks in smoke and elegies?

Who wants to sleep with a tomb
wake up next to so many dead bodies?

Who could love a thing that's always burning?

THE POET'S EULOGY

PASTOR HUGHES OF CONCORD BAPTIST CHURCH,
ROXBURY, MA

Blessed be the glory of God. Let the church say Amen.

Amen.

Though we are gathered here in mourning, today is a day He made and so we give thanks.

Mm-hm.

From what I hear of the woman Simone became, that's what she would've wanted. She would've wanted us to find a reason to give thanks.

Yes, Lord.

I didn't know her well as an adult, but I know she's Katie Days' grandbaby. Katie has graced this church with her voice for the past six decades, as she will again today later in the program.

Mm-hm.

I know she is the daughter of Phyllis and Gary John, who I married here back in '84. And I watched their family grow till they needed their own pew. Baptized Camille and Gary Jr. Christened Chanelle and Simone.

Yes, Jesus.

See, Concord was part of their lives before they were born. I prayed over Phyllis' belly in the hospital. Some of y'all were there.

Mm-hm.

I prayed God would bring two healthy babies into this world. Prayed His will was their survival. And it was. They arrived months before they should have. But if you know the girls, you know they do everything at their own pace.

Yes, Lord.

And that pace is usually quicker than we expect.

Ain't that right.

Simone did so much so young. Like she knew the clock's hands weren't ticking in her favor. And from where we're standing, it looks like she might've been right. But Christ said, *Do not let your hearts be troubled.* We know better than to let despair sink its teeth into our skin. We know that this is ultimately part of God's plan.

Yes Jesus, sweet Jesus.

And for that reason we will not descend into grief.
We will not dwell on the way this child's life was stolen.

Lord, help us. Dear Lord.
Someone go stand by Katie,
give her something to lean on.

We will lift her name in prayer.
We will speak her name aloud.
We will start now.

TESTIFY

TRAYVON MARTIN TESTIMONY POEMS TRANSCRIBED FROM VIDEOS FOUND AT: HTTP://
BIT.LY/TRAYVONAXIOMAMNESIA.

"SMALL TALK" COMMENTS ORIGINALLY FOUND AT: HTTP://BIT.LY/SMALLTALKCOMMENTS,
HTTP://BIT.LY/TRAYVONAXIOMAMNESIA.

"THE RETREAT AT TWIN LAKES" PROPERTY DESCRIPTION ORIGINALLY FOUND AT: HTTP://
BIT.LY/EASYSTREETREALTY.

THE FOLLOWING KENDRICK LAMAR ALBUMS/SONGS WERE REFERENCED:
GOOD KID, M.A.A.D CITY, TOP DAWG ENTERTAINMENT, 2012 (ALBUM);
"GOOD KID," TOP DAWG ENTERTAINMENT, 2012 (SONG);
"M.A.A.D. CITY," TOP DAWG ENTERTAINMENT, 2012 (SONG); AND
"SHERANE, AKA MASTER SPLINTER'S DAUGHTER,"
TOP DAWG ENTERTAINMENT, 2012 (SONG).

DIALOGUE IN "RACHEL'S EARRINGS" TAKEN FROM GEORGE ZIMMERMAN'S DEFENSE
ATTORNEY DON WEST.

"FROM" AND "446" ARE WRITTEN AFTER "FROM" AND "JOHN MONTIERE: ANSWER TO
QUESTION TWO" IN M-A-C-N-O-L-I-A, BY A. VAN JORDAN (2004).

SANDRA BLAND POEMS EXCERPTED FROM TRANSCRIPT FOUND AT: BIT.LY/
COLLATERALTRANSCRIPT.

"A BRIEF HISTORY OF MURDER" IS WRITTEN AFTER "THE LAST NEW YEAR'S RESOLUTION" BY KAZUMI CHIN.

"THINGS I DON'T SAY TO THE WHITE AUDIENCE AT THE POETRY READING" IS FOR KRYSTEN HILL

"ONLY EVERYTHING I OWN" IS WRITTEN AFTER PATRICIA SMITH'S POEM OF THE SAME TITLE.

"BURNING" EPIGRAPH TAKEN FROM DANEZ SMITH'S POEM, "SONG OF THE WRECKAGE".

MANY THANKS TO THE EDITORS OF *ELOHI GADUGI JOURNAL*, *WILDNESS*, AND *PUBLIC POOL* FOR PUBLISHING EARLY VERSIONS OF THE POEMS CONTAINED IN THIS BOOK. A PORTION OF THESE POEMS APPEARED IN A CHAPBOOK, *COLLATERAL*, PUBLISHED BY OCTOPUS BOOKS IN 2016.

THANKS TO THE DREAM TEAM AT OCTOPUS BOOKS FOR BELIEVING IN THIS WORK.

FOR THEIR FRIENDSHIP, MENTORSHIP, AND CONTINUED SUPPORT, THANK YOU TO: ELENA GEORGIOU, DARRAH CLOUD, NIKOLA MORRIS, MORGAN LINDSEY TACHCO, REI CHAMPION, KRYSTEN HILL, AMANDA TORRES, ASHLEY DAVIS, CASSANDRA CACOQ, RANDY SHINN, THE STAFF, FACULTY, AND STUDENTS AT GODDARD COLLEGE, AND SO MANY MORE. I AM BLESSED TO KNOW Y'ALL.

TO MY FAMILY: PHYLLIS JOHN, GARY JOHN SR., CAMILLE CLARK, GARY JOHN JR., STEPHANIE LAMB, DIANE SWAIN, LAWAN SWAIN, ĀZAR SWAIN, MAVIS HAWKINS, ROSHAUN HAWKINS, JENEE HAWKINS, KATIE DAYS, IVORY SWAIN, AND MANY OTHERS. I AM GRATEFUL FOR, AND HUMBLED BY, YOUR LOVE.

AND TO CHANELLE JOHN: BEING A TWIN IS ALL THE PROOF I NEED TO KNOW LIFE IS SACRED. THANKS FOR PAYING MY SUBMISSION FEES SO *TESTIFY* COULD HAVE A SPINE.